# A Kid's Guide to Drawing America™

# How to Draw
# Indiana's
## Sights and Symbols

Jenny Deinard

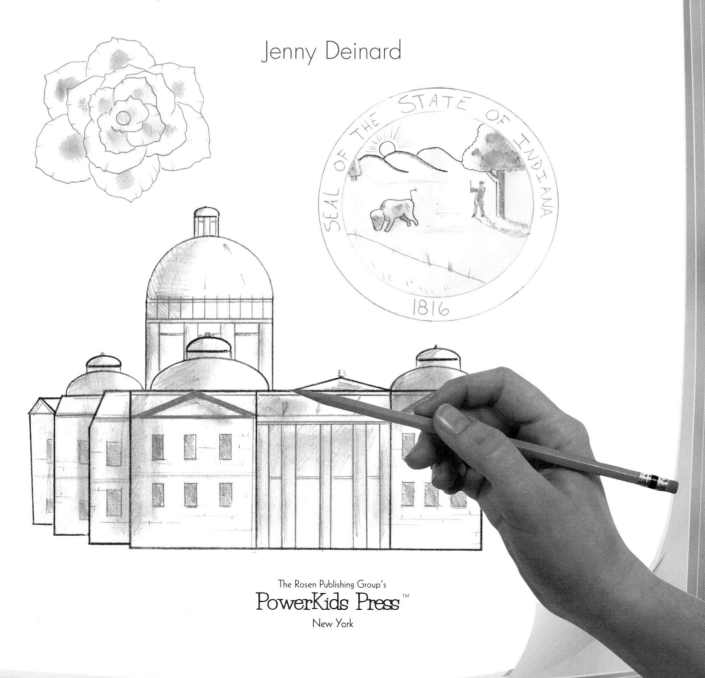

The Rosen Publishing Group's
PowerKids Press™
New York

*For the Grube Family*

Published in 2002 by The Rosen Publishing Group, Inc.
29 East 21st Street, New York, NY 10010

First Edition

Book Design: Kim Sonsky
Layout Design: Michael Donnellan
Project Editors: Jannell Khu, Jennifer Landau

Illustration Credits: p. 25 by Emily Muschinske, all other illustrations by Jamie Grecco.

Photo Credits: p. 7 © David Muench/CORBIS; pp. 8, 9 Tippecanoe County Historical Association, Lafayette, Indiana. Gift of Mrs. Cable G. Ball; pp. 12, 14 © One Mile Up, Incorporated; p. 16 © Wolfgang Kaehler/CORBIS; p. 18 © Christine Osborne/CORBIS; pp. 20, 24 © Index Stock; p. 26 courtesy of the Levi Coffin House Association; p. 28 © Stephen Sellers.

Deinard, Jenny
     How to draw Indiana's sights and symbols / Jenny Deinard
       p. cm — (A kid's guide to drawing America)
     Includes index.
     Summary: This book describes how to draw some of Indiana's sights and symbols, including the state's seal, the state's flag, the Indiana Motor Speedway, and others.
     ISBN 0-8239-6070-6
     1. Emblems. State—Indiana—Juvenile literature  2. Indiana in art—Juvenile literature
3. Drawing—Technique—Juvenile literature [1. Emblems, State—Indiana  2. Indiana  3. Drawing—Technique]
     I. Title II. Series
      2001
     743'.8'09772—dc21

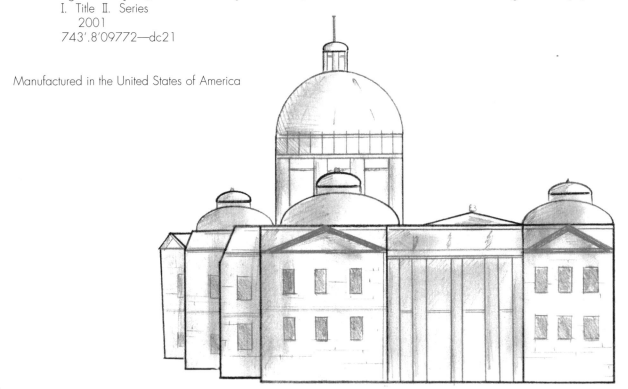

# CONTENTS

| 1 | Let's Draw Indiana | 4 |
| 2 | The Hoosier State | 6 |
| 3 | Artist in Indiana | 8 |
| 4 | Map of Indiana | 10 |
| 5 | The State Seal | 12 |
| 6 | The State Flag | 14 |
| 7 | The Peony | 16 |
| 8 | The Tulip Tree | 18 |
| 9 | The Cardinal | 20 |
| 10 | The Cannelton Cotton Mill | 22 |
| 11 | The Indianapolis Motor Speedway | 24 |
| 12 | Levi Coffin House | 26 |
| 13 | Indiana's Capitol | 28 |
| | Indiana State Facts | 30 |
| | Glossary | 31 |
| | Index | 32 |
| | Web Sites | 32 |

# Let's Draw Indiana

Indiana was given its name in 1800, when the U.S. Congress created the Indiana Territory. Indiana also is known as the Hoosier State. No one really knows how it got this nickname, but there are plenty of theories, some of which are pretty funny. One popular theory is that when early settlers in Indiana passed the homes of other settlers, they would call out, "Who's here?"

Industries in Indiana produce steel, transportation equipment, drug and chemical products, machinery, petroleum, and coal. The motto for the state is the Crossroads of America because it is located near the center of the country, and a crossroads is a central meeting place. Indiana also produces many crops on its land including corn, soybeans, hogs, poultry, eggs, cattle, and dairy products.

This book can help you to learn about some of Indiana's sights and symbols and how to draw them. All the drawings begin with a basic shape. You will then keep adding more shapes to the first shape. Directions help explain how to do every step. New steps of the drawing are shown in red to help guide you. Drawing terms also are provided to show you some of the shapes and words used in this book. Some of the drawings require shading. To shade just tilt your pencil to the side and hold it with your index finger. The most important thing to remember is to have fun!

You will need the following supplies to draw Indiana's sights and symbols:

- A sketch pad
- An eraser

- A number 2 pencil
- A pencil sharpener

These are some of the shapes and drawing terms you need to know to draw Indiana's sights and symbols:

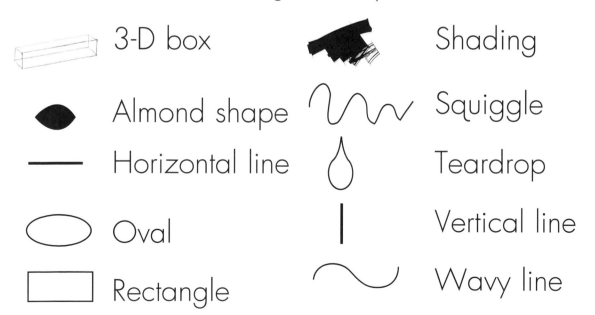

3-D box       Shading

Almond shape      Squiggle

Horizontal line      Teardrop

Oval      Vertical line

Rectangle      Wavy line

# The Hoosier State

Indiana was part of the Indiana Territory while it was owned by the United States. It became a state on December 11, 1816.

The six regions of Indiana are eastern, central, south-central, southern, western, and northern. Each area boasts its own scenic wonders. Native Hoosiers and tourists alike enjoy visiting the Whitewater Gorge Park, which is an old settlement with waterfalls, cliffs, and stone quarries, the Cecil M. Harden Lake, which is surrounded by many species of trees, wildflowers, berries, and mushrooms, and the Atterbury Fish and Wildlife Area, a 6,400-acre (2,590-ha) property which contains 200 acres (81 ha) of marshland. Brown County State Park is a popular location for campers and those who love the outdoors. Brown County is also home to a large colony of artists and craftspeople.

Indiana has few mountains or hilly areas. The Hoosier National Forest, however, is in a hilly area of south-central Indiana.

# Artist in Indiana

Artist George Winter

Like many great painters, George Winter was self-taught. In 1809, he was born in Portsea, today part of Portsmouth, England, and he was the youngest of 12 children. He was introduced to art by local artists and craftspeople. Young George stayed in England when his father and five of his siblings moved to America. When he moved to London at the age of 17, he visited the city's museums and art galleries. By copying the works of the world's master painters, he improved his artistic skill and talent.

George Winter made black-and-white sketches before he painted a scene.

Winter sailed to America in 1830. While living in the Midwest, Winter encountered the first Native Americans he had ever seen. Native Americans and their culture fascinated him. They influenced Winter's life and his work. Native Americans had been forced to give up their land and move west during the Indian Removal Act of 1830. Many of George Winter's works of art documented this painful event in American history. One example is his watercolor painting of a Native American family camped along a creek in Indiana.

This is a watercolor painting by George Winter titled *Pottawattamie Indians Crooked Creek, Indiana 1837.*

# Map of Indiana

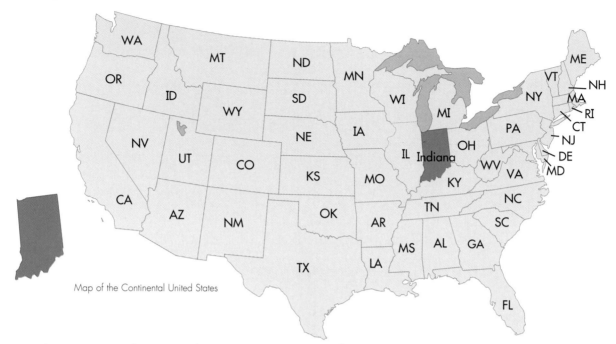

Map of the Continental United States

Indianapolis is the capital of Indiana and has a population of almost 750,000. Indiana covers 36,420 square miles (94,327 sq km) of land and borders Michigan, Ohio, Kentucky, and Illinois. The shores of Lake Michigan, one of the Great Lakes, are part of Indiana's northwest border. The Wabash River, popular in poetry and songs, flows from Ohio and crosses the state of Indiana to form part of the Indiana-Illinois border. Indiana has one national forest, the Hoosier National Forest. The Indiana Dunes National Lakeshore, along the southern edge of Lake Michigan, is a beautiful stretch of land covered with huge sand dunes. Hoosier Hill, Indiana's highest point at 1,257 feet (383 m), is near the Ohio border.

**1**

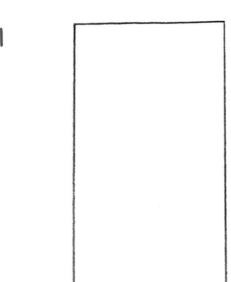

Start your drawing of Indiana by drawing a rectangle.

**3**

Erase extra lines.

**2**

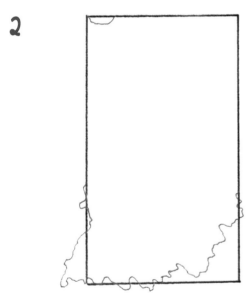

Using the rectangle as a guide, draw the shape of Indiana.

**4**

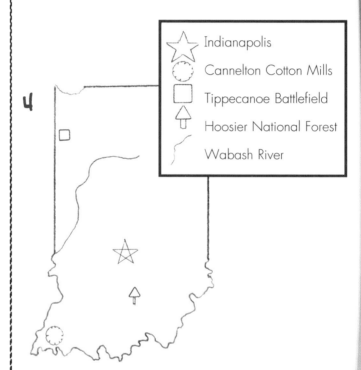

☆ Indianapolis

◌ Cannelton Cotton Mills

▢ Tippecanoe Battlefield

⌂ Hoosier National Forest

〰 Wabash River

a. Draw a circle to mark the Cannelton Cotton Mills.
b. Draw a square to show the Tippecanoe Battlefield.
c. Use a triangle and a rectangle to mark Hoosier National Forest.
d. Use a wavy line to draw the Wabash River.
e. Draw a star to mark Indiana's capital, Indianapolis.

# The State Seal

Indiana adopted its state seal in 1963. "Seal of the State of Indiana" and "1816," the date that Indiana became a state, are written around the border of the state seal. In the center of the seal is a scene showing an Indiana landscape. This scene shows the bright sun above the hills in the distance, and two sycamore trees on the right side of the seal. There is an image of a buffalo, which once roamed the plains of Indiana in great numbers. A woodsman is shown holding an ax, ready to cut down a tree. The seal recalls a time when many pioneers heading west decided to settle and stay in Indiana.

**1**

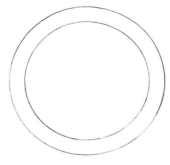

Start by drawing two large circles, one inside the other.

**2**

In the inner circle, add two rectangles to form a branch and the trunk of a tree.

**3**

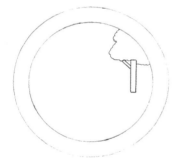

Draw the outline of the tree's leaves using a wavy line.

**4**

Add the hills in the back using curved lines.

**5**

Draw a circle for the sun at the top of the hills, and wavy lines for sunrays. Add a wavy line at the bottom.

**6**

Add four small circles to begin your drawing of the buffalo.

**7**

Using the circles as guides, draw in the buffalo, adding its legs and tail. Begin to draw the woodsman's body, legs, head and hat.

**8**

Draw the man's arms and his ax. Add shading to the seal. Erase extra lines. Add the year "1816" and the words "SEAL OF THE STATE OF INDIANA."

# The State Flag

The Indiana state flag was designed by Paul Hadley, a resident of Mooresville, Indiana. Lawmakers in the state government voted to adopt this flag design in 1917. The flag has a deep blue background. The design shows a flaming, golden torch and 19 gold stars. The outer circle of 13 stars represents the nation's first 13 colonies. Five additional stars represent the next five states admitted to the Union. Above the torch and its flame is a large star, which represents Indiana, the nineteenth state.

**1**

Start by drawing a rectangle.

**2**

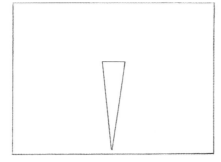

Draw a triangle for the torch.

**3**

Add two thin rectangles to the torch.

**4**

Draw in shapes for the flame as shown.

**5**

Separate the center of the torch by redrawing the four-sided shape. Make sure there are spaces between the top and the bottom.

**6**

Add six lines coming off of the flame.

**7**

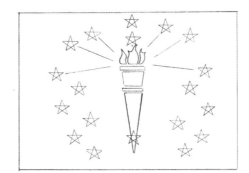

Draw 19 stars as shown. Make the center star larger to represent Indiana.

**8**

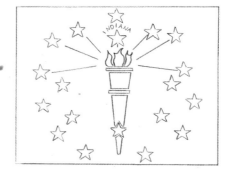

Erase extra lines within stars. Write in the word "INDIANA."

# The Peony

Indiana has had five different state flowers! The tulip tree blossom was the state flower in the 1870s. In 1913, the state flower was changed to the carnation. Then the state flower was changed back to the tulip tree blossom. In 1931, the flower was changed to the zinnia. In 1957, many flowers were considered for a new official Indiana state flower. On March 13 of that year, the peony was chosen. Many people believed that an Indiana state lawmaker influenced the decision since he grew peonies. The peony blooms in May and June. It has a beautiful, fragrant smell and appears in many shades, from dark pink to white.

**1**

Start by drawing a circle for the center of the flower.

**2**

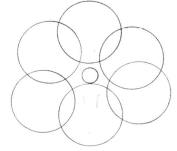

Then add six large circles around the center of the flower. It's fine if they overlap.

**3**

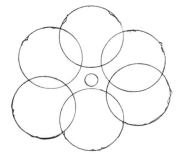

Using the circles as guides, draw the shape of the petals.

**4**

Erase extra lines, and draw five half circles around the center of the flower.

**5**

You can start drawing the shapes of the petals by using the half circles as guides.

**6**

Erase extra lines and add six more half circles to the center of the flower.

**7**

Using the half circles as guides, draw the shapes of the petals.

**8**

Erase any extra lines. Add shading and detail to your flower and you're done.

# The Tulip Tree

On March 3, 1931, the tulip tree (*Liriodenron tulipifera*) became Indiana's state tree. Tulip trees are also known as yellow poplars. The tree has greenish white flowers. These trees were once found commonly throughout Indiana, but logging for timber has reduced the number of tulip trees in the state. Tulip trees can grow to be more than 200 feet (61 m) tall, although the average tree of this species is about 150 feet (46 m) tall. Their trunks can reach 12 feet (4 m) in diameter. Today the wood from tulip trees is used often to make furniture.

**1**

Start by drawing a rectangle.

**2**

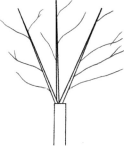

To draw branches, draw three very thin triangles that point out from the rectangle.

**3**

Draw wavy lines to add branches that come out from the thin triangles.

**4**

Draw six circles over the branches.

**5**

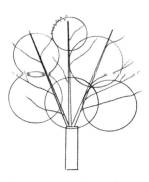

Using the circles as guides, draw the leaves using V shapes.

**6**

Erase all the lines inside the circles.

**7**

Add shading and detail to your tree. Erase any extra smudges and you're done.

# The Cardinal

The cardinal became Indiana's state bird in 1933. Cardinals can be heard singing happy-sounding songs, and their trills usually last for about three seconds. The male and female cardinals have different plumage. The male cardinal is a beautiful, bright red color with black around his eyes and beak. The female cardinal is pale brown with a reddish tint. Both male and female cardinals have a crest of plumes on their heads. Cardinals are from 7 ½ to 8 inches (19–20 cm) long including their 4-inch (10-cm) tail. Cardinals build their nests off the ground in bushes and shrubs. Female cardinals lay three or four white eggs with brown, speckled markings. They eat insects, grains, wild fruit, and seeds. They especially like sunflower seeds.

**1**

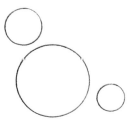

Start by drawing three circles for the bird's head and body.

**2**

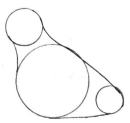

Then connect the circles with a curved line that circles the body.

**3**

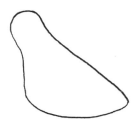

Erase any extra lines.

**4**

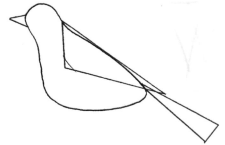

Draw three triangles, a tiny one for the beak, one for the wing, and one for the bird's tail.

**5**

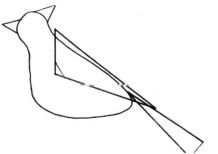

Draw a triangle for the bird's head feathers.

**6**

Use four lines to draw the bird's legs.

**7**

Draw a small circle for an eye and use six lines for the bird's feet.

**8**

To finish your bird, add detail and shading. You can use your finger to smudge the pencil lines.

21

# The Cannelton Cotton Mill

The Cannelton Cotton Mill was one of the largest and most beautiful buildings built before the Civil War. When the Indiana textile industry wanted to compete with successful mills in New England, local businessmen and landowners teamed up with investors from New England to build the mill in Cannelton. It was completed in 1851. The mill faces the north bank of the Ohio River. It is a long, narrow building with two towers on each side of the main entrance. The mill produced textiles from 1851 to 1954. It has a fascinating history that includes making uniforms for men fighting in the Civil War and other textiles for both world wars. In 1976, the mill was included in the National Register of Historic Places.

**1**

Start by drawing a long rectangle for the shape of the building.

**2**

Then add two smaller rectangles at each end of the large one.

**3**

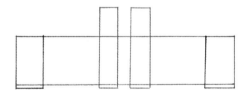

Draw two long, narrow rectangles at the center of the building to form its towers.

**4**

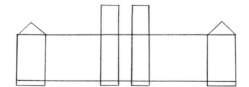

Draw two triangles to add roofs for the rectangles at each end of the building.

**5**

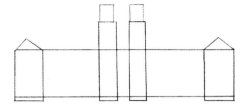

Add two rectangles on top of the center towers.

**6**

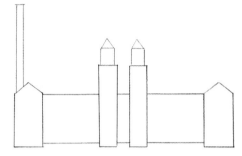

Draw a long, thin rectangle to make a smokestack. Add two triangles on top of the center towers. Erase extra lines.

**7**

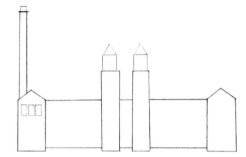

Draw in three rectangles for windows. Add a small rectangle to the top of the smokestack.

**8**

Draw in all remaining windows. Add shading and detail. Erase any extra smudges and you're done. You can also add smoke coming from the smokestack.

# The Indianapolis Motor Speedway

In the spring of 1909, the Indianapolis Motor Speedway was built on 328 acres (133 ha) of Indiana farmland. It was created by four businessmen who wanted to test-drive cars. More than three million bricks, most now paved over, were used to build the speedway, and it became known as "the brickyard." The Yard of Bricks is a portion of the original track that is still exposed. When auto racing became a popular sport, the first 500-mile (8054-km) auto race took place at the Speedway in 1911. Ray Harroun won $14,240 in prize money. Today this famous race is called the Indianapolis 500, or the Indy 500. The stands can seat 250,000 people, which makes the speedway the largest sports arena in the world.

**1**

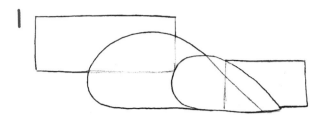

Begin by looking at the car and breaking it down into its basic shapes. You can use two rectangles and two teardrops on their sides.

**2**

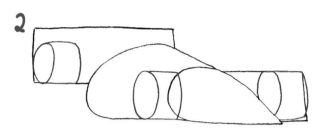

Add three wheels. The fourth wheel is hidden behind the car.

**3**

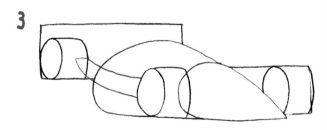

Add the shape that stretches from the front to the back wheel.

**4**

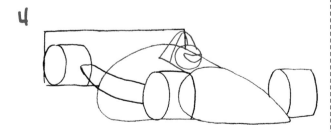

Draw the racecar driver's head. He's wearing a helmet. Draw the protective arch that rises above his head. This arch protects him if the car rolls over. Erase the extra line connecting the right wheel to the car.

**5**

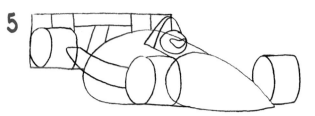

Add the rear area of the car. It is made using a series of rectangular shapes.

**6**

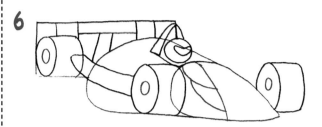

Add the details to the front of the car. They are made using arcs. Add the circles inside each wheel.

**7**

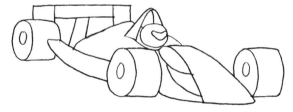

Erase all of the extra lines. You have a clean outline of the racecar.

**8**

Shade the car. You can add extra details if you like. Some racecars have fancy paint jobs with stripes and fire.

# Levi Coffin House

The Levi Coffin House in Fountain City, Indiana, was once an important station in the Underground Railroad. The Underground Railroad was a system of secret routes and houses that African Americans used to escape from slavery in the South. In 1826, Levi Coffin, an important merchant, built an eight-room house in the town of Newport (now called Fountain City), Indiana. Levi and his wife, Catherine, were Quakers and abolitionists. They made their home a "train stop" for the "passengers," who fled from slavery. The Coffins may have helped more than 2,000 people to freedom. Visitors to the Levi Coffin House are shown the secret rooms where "passengers" on the Underground Railroad were hidden.

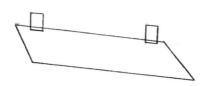

1

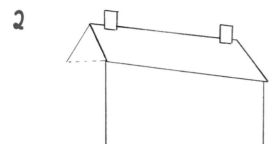

Start by drawing a large, slanted rectangle for the shape of the roof, and two small rectangles for the chimneys.

2

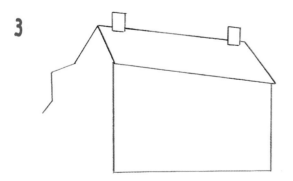

Add two lines to make a triangle for the slanted roof. Make the bottom line dotted. Draw a rectangle for the front of the building.

3

Add three short lines for the back side of the building. Erase the dotted line in the triangle.

4

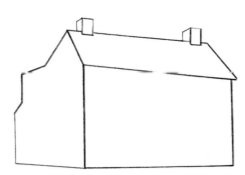

Connect the back and front of the building with two lines. Add two small, slanted rectangles to the chimneys to add depth.

5

Use rectangles to draw the doors and windows.

6

Add shading and detail to your building. Erase any extra smudges and you're done. You can also add a flag.

# Indiana's Capitol

On September 28, 1880, a 10-ton (9-t) block of Indiana limestone, inscribed with the words "A.D. 1880," was laid as the cornerstone of Indiana's state capitol. The first state house was built in 1830, at the cost of about $60,000. When the roof leaked every time it rained and the walls began to crumble, lawmakers voted to build a new state capitol. They insisted that it cost no more than $2 million. The new Indiana state capitol was completed on October 2, 1888. Many people said that it resembled the U.S. Capitol in Washington, D.C. One hundred years later, in 1988, Indiana celebrated its capitol's centennial. This time it cost $11 million to restore the building.

**1**

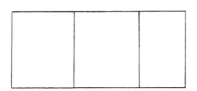

Start by drawing three large rectangles for the front of the building.

**2**

Add three shapes to the side of the building as shown.

**3**

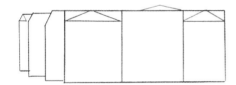

Add four triangles.

**4**

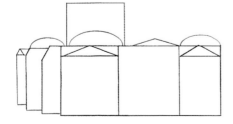

Add another rectangle for the base of the dome, and three half ovals.

**5**

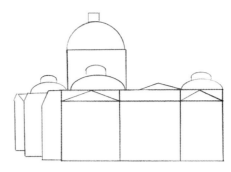

Add three more half ovals and a half circle for the dome. Then place a small rectangle on top of the dome.

**6**

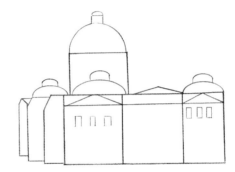

Draw a small half oval on top and draw your windows using rectangles.

**7**

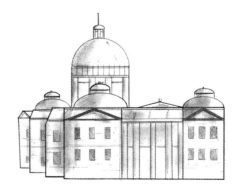

Add shading and detail to your building. Erase any extra smudges and you're done.

# Indiana State Facts

| | |
|---|---|
| Statehood | December 11, 1816, 19th state |
| Area | 36,420 square miles (94,328 sq km) |
| Population | 5,942,900 |
| Capital | Indianapolis, population 746,700 |
| Most Populated City | Indianapolis |
| Industries | Transportation equipment, steel, coal, pharmaceutical and chemical products |
| Agriculture | Corn, soybeans, hogs, poultry, and eggs |
| Tree | Tulip tree |
| Poem | "Indiana" by Arthur Franklin Mapes |
| Motto | The Crossroads of America |
| Nickname | The Hoosier State |
| Bird | Cardinal |
| Flower | Peony |
| Stone | Limestone |
| River | Wabash River |
| Song | "On the Banks of the Wabash, Far Away" by Paul Dresser |
| Language | English and American Sign Language |

# Glossary

**abolitionists** (a-buh-LIH-shun-ists)  Men and women who wanted to end slavery.

**adopted** (uh-DOPT-ed)  To have accepted or approved something.

**centennial** (sen-TEH-nee-ul)  Relating to a one-hundredth anniversary.

**Civil War** (SIH-vul WOR)  The war fought between the northern and southern states of America from 1861 to 1865.

**crest** (KREST)  A head decoration on a bird.

**diameter** (dy-A-meh-tur)  The measurement across the center of a round object.

**fascinated** (FA-sin-ayt-ed)  Very interested.

**fragrant** (FRAY-grint)  Pleasant smelling.

**investors** (in-VES-turz)  People who support something by giving money.

**lawmakers** (LAW-may-kurz)  People who write and pass laws.

**marshland** (MARSH-land)  Low, wet land.

**petroleum** (peh-TROH-lee-um)  An oily liquid found beneath the surface of Earth that can be used to make gasoline and other products.

**plumage** (PLOO-mij)  A bird's feathers.

**Quakers** (KWAY-kurz)  People who belong to a religion that believes in equality for all people, strong families and communities, and peace.

**quarries** (KWOR-eez)  Areas of land where stones for building can be found.

**register** (REH-jih-ster)  An official record book.

**species** (SPEE-sheez)  A single kind of plant or animal. For example, all people are one species.

**symbols** (SIM-bulz)  Objects or designs that stand for something important.

**textile** (TEK-styl)  Woven fabric or cloth.

**theories** (THEE-uh-reez)  Ideas that try to explain something.

**timber** (TIM-bur)  Wood that is cut and used for building houses, ships, and other wooden objects.

**trills** (TRILZ)  Birdsong.

# Index

**A**
Atterbury Fish and
    Wildlife Area, 6

**B**
Brown County State
    Park, 6

**C**
Cannelton Cotton
    Mill, 22
carnation, 16
Cecil M. Harden
    Lake, 6
Civil War, 22

**H**
Hadley, Paul, 14
Harroun, Ray, 24
Hoosier, 4

Hoosier Hill, 10
Hoosier National
    Forest, 10

**I**
Indiana Territory, 4, 6
Indian Removal Act of
    1830, 9

**L**
Levi Coffin House, 26

**N**
National Register of
    Historic Places, 22

**O**
Ohio River, 22

**S**
state bird, 20
state flag, 14

state flower, 16
state seal, 12

**T**
Tulip tree, 18

**U**
Underground
    Railroad, 26

**W**
Wabash River, 10
Whitewater Gorge
    Park, 6
Winter, George, 8, 9

**Z**
zinnia, 16

# Web Sites

To find out more about Indiana, check out this Web site:
www.state.in.us